Threads of a Life

A Journey Woven Over Time

Smita Amit

INDIA • UK • USA

Paperback: 978-93-6926-093-5

eBook: 978-93-6926-135-2

First Published in January, 2026

Published by Walnut Publication

(an imprint of Vyusta Platforms Private Limited)

www.walnutpublication.com

India

Unit# 909, 9th Floor, Wave Silver Tower, Sector-18, Noida - 201301

UK

71-75 Shelton Street, Covent Garden, London, WC2H 9JQ, UK

Distributed by

Dedicated to my deeply learned father, Professor (Dr.) A. S. Narain, who nurtured my love for poetry, recognized and encouraged my creative voice, and helped me navigate life's highs and lows; and to my devoted mother, Dr. Bandana Narain, who instilled in me the priceless lesson of resilience and strength.

Table of Contents

The Unsung Genius 1
A Eulogy 3
One Persona 5
A Silent, Helpless Watch........ 7
Ahoy 9
Suspiration........ 11
Alas! That was years ago 13
Allure? 15
An Inquest 18
And She Fights On 20
Anguish! From Heaven 22
It Is That Time of the Year Again 24
Balance 26
Centuries Apart, Still 28
Elixir of Dreams 30
Emotions........ 32
Ergo, They Wait........ 34
Kinks in the Armour 35
If – A Woman's Cry 37
In Shambles... 38
Incarcerated 39
The Edge of Forgiveness 40
Love 41
Magic........ 43

O Just Sometimes 45
Nature- the Eternal Mystic 47
You !! 49
Fate Bends Not 51
O' Autumn 53
On the Train, Once Again 54
And Yet She Waited 55
Looking for Bliss 57
Reincarnation 59
Silence 60
Stifled 61
Silhouette's 63
Tales and Lessons – The Web 64
The Childhood Still Waits 66
The Day the Song Died 68
Ruins 71
The Bleeding Heart 73
The Dive 74
The Nilgiris 76
The Knot in My Temple 77
Violence in Me 78
The Martyr 81
No Throw for Her 82
The Legacy 85
Strength 88
My Tryst with Poetry and Prose 89

The Unsung Genius

Smita Amit

Dedicated to my Genius Father

He bore a voice both rich and deep,
A hand that painted, bold yet neat.
A greater man I've yet to find,
And none so simple, pure in mind.

Decades have been spent,
The famed genius brain behind.
The weight, the slant, the bent,
The reason—hoping to find.

But then, as said Stephen Gould,
Interesting it is to look for the certainty
That akin brains out there in the cold
Live and pass away unknown for eternity.

Brains that the world knew not ever,
Caught as it is in petty games of shows.
Perhaps those minds were far more clever,
Alas, perishing, employed in simple chores.

Tilling cornfields, or the humble scholar,
Whom fame—this world denied.
Went away simply, without a murmur,
He did his work well, ne'er complained nor cried.

One such man, my darling father,
A greater man I have yet to find.
Like him, there will perhaps be no other,
In him, genius and talents together did rescind.

To all such minds, lost yet grand,
Who shaped the world with unseen hands—
I bow to you, the quiet few,
Whose light still shines, though none yet knew.

A Eulogy

Smita Amit (8/1/1990)

That empty corner, redolent —
Serene walls buried deep,
Tranquil, in silence eloquent,
The vacant space asleep.

Unfazed — a speck of calm,
Not ruffled, nor losing its sheen —
While I, in the whirlpool of desire,
With hustling, churning thoughts,
And in a tussle, my emotions on fire.

As the dust of shattered, broken illusions
Keeps maiming and crushing —
My innards gripped in tangled confusions —
But it remains like Shangri-La — evocative,
In its warm confines,
Giving me the courage to again live.
Like the laze of winking rosebuds,
Like resplendent skies,
Adorned with a thousand studs —
Bright with a thousand hues,
It drives away
My pains and my blues.

But for its solitary contours,
Where my spirit wanders —
Free, flying in the moors,
It's comforting, downy insides —
My refuge, my kinsman —
In it, my existence, hope resides.
O empty corner of my heart,
If not for you — my harbour —
My succour, my saviour thou art.
My life, its serenity —
I owe to thee.

You help me through all calamity.
Erudition of survival you impart —
Selflessly, O much-valued
Empty corner of my heart.

One Persona

Smita Amit

One persona, kaleidoscopic hues—
Man in bloom, bearing dues.
Defying laws for fleeting gold,
Reality knocks,
Truth unfolds.

Yes—Man must face his inner self.
No escape.
The mundane, the exorbitant,
The extravagant—hand in glove—
Now dapple the work that's done.

The maiden's fearlessness, courage, and silence
Rush to rescue.
Time, the soother,
The healer,
Will take its ledger.

The writing on the wall is bare:
From dust to dust—
And nothing more.

Footprints fade,
As many tales are told.

The universe blossoms after the rains.
There is hope
In humaneness still.

A Silent, Helpless Watch

Smita Amit 25/6/2025

The mysterious mist — silently eloquent —
Rising, nay wafting, slowly up the valleys,
Filling unseen spaces between shaggy mountains.
Unending narrow hill roads — blind bends.

The hot cuppa along the way, sizzling cozily,
Bouncing small and large streams and fountains.
The eerie silence of darkness on hills.

A faint light — a cottage far away.
The beetles, crickets — nature uncensored.
The pine-scented breeze the nostril fills.
The broad-leaved teak gently does sway.

The monal prancing, enchantingly feathered.
Mountain goats — their feast on slopes.
The drizzle that muzzles on window panes.
The acacia blooms, ferns refreshed.

Bewitching sunrise, activating all folks,
Spilling, encompassing the gorge and yonder plains.
The mighty Ra — all over, his rays enmeshed.

But the silence remains — beautifully thoughtful —
To the kin of earth and sky belonging.
The mountain ash, its flowers violet-mauve.

Zya-zya goes the olive-green crested bulbul.
Avocado foliage — the glades shining.
Frank, open nature — nothing suave.
Scurrying black weasels crossing the path,
The slow, steady aphid in its routine engrossed.
The mist, a pour now — the skies overcast.
Sounds pristine, unleashed — His pen hath.
The marten siblings collect food before the frost.
The spotting of creatures moving slow or fast.

Sitting in stillness on the mountain ridge,
I watch the play of the Creator's brush.
The spruce and oak bowing to the nectar drop,
And moss or the fir leaves that gently squidge.

Amazing, enthralling — the indigo bush.
Sadly, indestructible man-made articles also pop...
For amidst this grace, man's greed lies strewn —
Felled birch lies mute on the mangled slope,
Dust swirls where wildflowers should be.

The brick and steel are spreading too soon,
Gnawing through nature, cutting off hope —
Tarnishing beauty we once held free.

Will this evil design go unabated,
Smothering all in a ravenous gust?
Who on earth shall this avarice bolt, alas?
Will the wisdom of the wise be conflated?
Ye mankind — if not, then annihilate we must —
Of what worth then, this wealth you amass?

Ahoy

Smita Amit January 2025

A rivulet slid from her lashes' brim,
A tide of sorrow, soft and dim.
No hand reached out, no kindred grace
To still the storm time can't erase.

She drowned not just in waves or rain,
But in echoes of a long-lost name.
The silence roared, too loud to bear,
Her breath a gasp in hollow air.

A barren stretch her heart now treads,
Footprints trailing all that's fled.
Each tear — a chronicle, unsaid,
Of dreams that died but never bled.

They gathered round with laughter thin,
Blind to the tempest churning within.
Their mirth a cruel and brittle gleam,
A fragile dance on shattered dreams.

But she — her sail, her compass, her core,
Still rides the winds to distant shore.
Her faith, a stone beneath the tide,
Her love a fire she cannot hide.

His voice — a hush inside the breeze,
His absence deeper than the seas.
Yet still she stands, though weathered, worn,
A lighthouse dim, by mourning torn.

Let vultures crave her spirit's wane,
She shines — through darkness, through the rain.
Her grief, her strength, an unseen roar —
Ahoy, she cries, I break no more.

Suspiration

Smita Amit (1987)

With my solitude for company
And silence the only sound,
Myself the sole occupant,
I gaze from the window, looking far beyond.

I am one with the greenery
And at peace with the flowers.
Suddenly the sky seems to sing,
And pouring come the showers.

The earth seems resplendent,
Birds all merry and prancing,
Pathways washed and cleaned,
Shod by green — its splendid sheen.

The swinging, dancing leaves
Like waves in the sea,
And the lazy little rosebud
Has lazily winked at me.

All this beauty around me
Fills me with joyous wonder.
The golden smiling sunrays
Stun me with blinding splendor.

Dancing thus come my thoughts —
Them all I wish to share,
As deep in them am I lost,
Missing a kin who would care.

A mate, a twin even perhaps,
For nature has spread its ware,
And amidst this glorious beauty,
I just wish — he were there.

Alas! That was years ago

Reason it seems, woefully left him
The winds forgetting to blow
Enchanting melodies suddenly emanating
But alas! that was years ago.

Bent in work they stood apart
Then turned homeward to go
Sparks inexplicable suddenly ignited
But alas! that was years ago.

Whys wherefores filling all chatter
He had loved answering them so...
Lanes twinkled as he walked her home
But alas! that was years ago.

A local girl, and not his type
She was shielded by her kin, so...
Still his heart had beat for her
But alas! that was years ago.

No statement, no promise
Not even a letter to show
Yet acquiescing his willing heart
But alas! that was years ago.

Fate then turned woefully turtle
Not sure if he had let her go
Providence intervening with all its wiles
But then that was years ago.

Life then happened in all its fury
And riches did the maker bestow
Her waif-likepastels somewhat forgotten
After all, tis' was years ago.

In the twilight of life, wishes fulfilled
Basking in the throes of a heady ego
Her pastel scarf fluttered in, from lands beyond ...
Was it really ...years ago?

Allure?

Smita Amit

Allure: I wonder?
Conch-like eyes with glittering pearls,
A swaying gait — a jasmine bough.
Alabaster skin, lips like rose,
A delicate neck with a swan-like pose.

Their beauty unsurpassed:
Helen of Troy or Hina of Hawaii,
Famed across all shores,
Desired by many, courted by dozens and scores.

Spirited away across borders,
Traversing seas with turbulent tides.
By kings were they sought —
Countless battles, terrible wars fought.

Often enough, I wonder thus:
What did they feel? Whom did they love?
For whom did the butterflies flutter?
The fire in their innards flicker?
Was it the husband who commandeered,
Ordered and took as right?
Or the smitten lover who cherished every smile,
Treasuring them, lacking guile?
Did they suffer for anyone?
Did they allow themselves to feel?

Did the violins strum?
Did their hearts with ardor hum?
Did they mourn the lover ever —
The besotted, poor soul
Who loved a married woman thus,
And a mother plus?

Born was he a prince,
With the beauty of the realm all his.
He gave up empire, gave up life —
Laying it down for another man's wife.
One man stole; the other
Reclaimed, avenged, and killed — triumphant.
What in the depth of their hearts raged ever?
I contemplate. I chew over.
Did they exist, impassive —
Carrying on mundane chores?

Performing, escorts to the throne —
Their hearts merely turned to stone?
Is beauty born to simply suffer,
Or does she have a will?
Is she only an exquisite stiff,
That feels none of life's biff?

Appearing a windfall, a felicity,
A bliss that meets the marvelling eye —
But how many tempests, how much gust
Not feeling, hiding, must lie?
"A thing of beauty is a joy forever,"

With élan, this is quoted often.
But a joy for whom, I ponder —
The carrier, or the beholder?
Allure? Benefaction?
Alas, I often wonder... I do... I do...

An Inquest

Smita Amit: 18/5/21

Tethered,
Bewitching, the waters yonder,
Suspiring the waves, signal as they saunter
Mysterious,
The hills, the valleys
Clarion call blaring, the brooks and alleys
Fabled
The creatures winged or otherwise
Or volcanic lava, unforgiving that fries
Enticing
Mountain peaks, or forests pine
Bales of straw, grasslands and sunshine
Kingdoms
Just or cruel, vast or small
I want to visit, see, explore... them, all
Dreaming
Of a day still cosseted
In the womb of time, its arrival, coveted
Around me
But, lies the water muddy
Akin, the marsh, where I bob unsteady
Engulfing,
The slush, my discolored hull
Makes me feel, dreams are void and null

Shackled
Has a lifetime gone
Any breath left for a lustrous dawn?

Wondering
Even if the ropes be snipped and cut
Will my keel make it to the sublime hut,
Desuetude
My aging stern and bow
Can they now even, over the spume row?
The tides, their calling in the hours wee —
Alas! have they waited too long for me?

And She Fights On

Smita Amit (2005)

Inspired by the Jessica Lal case
In her eyes — ravished, raging — a forest fire,
Hark! it spells forth her ire.
A life so dear, lost to a gunshot mere?

The petition she filed, with not a fear,
Thinking her case was crystal clear.
Toiling her submission, fighting her plea,
Her eyes so green, like the turbulent sea.
Some deposed, but lies in a dozen,
Some not — their tongues forsaken.
Howling winds then in her eyes flew,
For justice, alas, had survived but few.
Months turned to years and more,
Possibilities all she did explore.
Deserted dunes — morbid and stifling —
Lay in now bereft eyes, silently rippling.
When the years had piled, all of seven,
Macabre a judgment, bemoaning even heaven.
Scot-free then they went, a-mocking,
Like pits the eyes, desolation flocking.

And then it came — a strange deluge,
Support unprecedented, a welcome refuge.
It came from all corners, from men unknown,

Sewing anew the hopes that were torn.
Shining now, her eyes strong and bright,
Kindled, sparkling — all ends alight.
The struggle she walked once more,
The law again she did implore.

Lies and more again fill the air,
As they seek to trap law, in cash and terror.
Beads of bewilderment clog her eyes,
Smoking, darkened, like snooty skies.

Eyes that were once the fetching azure
Will never be the same — that is for sure.
But will, in this land of the Goddess,
Women ever stop living in duress?

Will ever the Jessicas and many more
The atrocities of men no longer endure?
Will the law of our glorious land
Mete out justice, hold their hand?
Will the eyes of its fairer race
Be tranquil pools — or with anguish forever ablaze?

Anguish! From Heaven

Smita Amit (Jan 2003)

Inspired by the death of a young woman in the battalion whose husband cried bushels upon her death and remarried within a month

Was I ever
The smile in your dreams?
Did I form
Part of your life's many schemes?
Could I touch
The core of your heart, ever?
Was I one with you
In passion's deepest fervor?
Could I be
Ever in step with you—
As we walked,
Hands entwined in rosy hue?
Did you
Laugh and cry with me, truly?
Could I ever
Connect with you,willy-nilly?
Your love, companion, wife—
And more, was I.
Together, we had planned
To reach for the sky,
Wanting to be one—

Not me, not you, but *we*.
But now that truth
Lies bare to see.
For you, shrug, move on—
Our time together cast aside.
What lived with us
With me has died.
It **did** die.

It Is That Time of the Year Again

Smita Amit · 20/3/09

It is that time of the year again—
A vacuum where leaves float, wistfully away,
When the warmth of winter slowly gives way,
When the covers desert you at night,
The sun stings—no longer invitingly bright.

It is that time of the year again—
When clouds of dust begin to ascend,
And your spirits... *poof!*—suddenly descend.
The colors of spring appear sadly faded,
Even dew's bright twinkle seems jaded.

It is that time of the year again—
Many such years have passed me by,
Many such seasons have made me cry.
But rising from the ashes of pain and strife,
Like the phoenix, my soul has lived its life.

It is that time of the year again—
Each time, my childlike faith takes a beating,
My belief in paradise in measures retreating.

Still, I clutch at the fairies, the elves,
In the twinkling stars where joyfulness dwells.

If only it were that time of the year again—
When leaves no longer lie abandoned by the sire,
When the soul beams, knowing no ire,
When the blooms of spring bewitchingly smile,
And bliss reigns in a kingdom that stretches for many a
mile.

Balance

Smita Amit: 24/1/25

Little angels all around
Their antics, their play — enchanting.
Pranced in the playground, joy unbound.
There I sat, pensive, watching —
Innocence swaying on swings happily,
Or balancing the see-saw, laughing merrily.
I watched from afar, my spirits uplifted.

As up one went, down came the other,
Savouring the peace so simply gifted.
What if one weighed a ton, the other a feather?
On the zenith one, nadir the next —
The up, the down transpire — will not, on any pretext.
Like flowering buds, in clusters yonder
In times of spring, bright and yellow —
But think about this, do ponder:

What if the sun blazed or all was covered in snow?
The land then would be barren, mere —
For the divine balance wouldn't be there.
Like the gurgling stream, spritely,
With its enchanting melody filling the air,
Bouncing on rocks, pebbles —willy-nilly.
But what if boulders, big or small, weren't there?
Would there then be the beauteous sound, think?

The stream would, like a torrent, swipe without a blink.
The same is life — various aspects, big or small:
The blood coursing in the veins, the active brain —
They run on a pattern, balanced all —
The yin, the yang, the joy, the pain.
If they were one more than the other be,
The soul, the spirit would strain, then to flee.

Abundance of one, paucity of one —
Nature's delicate balance upset.
If it were just sunshine, would it be fun,
Lacking the warmth of fire the winter doth beset?
So cry not if sorrows seem more, unending,
For every cloud must hold — a silver lining.

Centuries Apart, Still

Smita Amit: 22/7/25

For him, it was grief, relief for her.
He wanted an answer, revenge even.
She wanted to break free and away go.
For him, it lingered; it ceased for her.
He wanted to confront — argue, even.
She had had enough and just needed to go.

Long ago, the two had met —
Still raw from love undone, she.
He stood lost, drowning in pity.
No skies broke open when they met.
He leaned forward; drew back — she.
He rose high; she sank in pity.

Caring, considerate he appeared — on face.
Needing help, to him turned she.
"I am good. I give," so believed he.
And thus, one day, a moment did they face —
Succumbing to his advances, she.
Then playing hard to get — suddenly, he.

Earlier, so vulnerable and sad seemed he.
Now the judge — driving her to tears.
Pleading, entreating, begging even — she.
Plaguing her with questions; unmoved stayed he.
As her strength returned, wiping the tears —
To move on and close it: deciding, she.

Cutting all ties — now resolute she was
Fickle-minded, his stance changed — he.
Bombarding her space, harassed was she.
"Come back — how could you?" his plea was.
Blaming her — abusing too — remained he.
But resolute her resolve; moving on, she.

“I am the victim — she, heartless, cruel!
I was willing — ready to take her in,
Ignoring her flaws — the great, forgiving me.”
Thinking thus, obsessing, he turned cruel.
He blamed it all — never once looked in.
“Cold. Corrupt. Her virtue in doubt. She left me.”

Toward revenge, with purpose, he strides.
Self-righteous, exalted — his shining armour.
Toward her — though she had blocked all roads.
But she, head high, in quiet strength strides.
“I deserve more” — that belief, her armour.
She charts her path toward welcoming roads.

Basking, preening — self-importance his staff.
Living in centuries past, entrapped.
He remains a man akin to men.
Secure in belief — her arrows, quiver, her staff.
She no longer in subjugation, entrapped.
Women have grown. Of old remain men.

Elixir of Dreams

Smita Amit: 31/7/2024

They thrashed — emerald, blue, and white,
The sea vast, held them, gently suspiring.
In rhythm, they sprinkled their salty sprite —
Playful, lazy, or active, never tiring.

Yonder flies the seagull, snowy, solitary,
Towards the lone relic, hanging forbidding,
On the granite cliff perched — ghostly, eerie —
The wasting bungalow, amongst seaweeds skidding.
What tales it holds? What is the lore?

I wonder, sitting on the mossy seashore,
The mind — a kaleidoscope — slips into reverie.
Hidden in dark alleys, and many a feathery cobweb,
Lie skeletons of men in sooty dungeons, rusty chains.
Did ever gigantic waves rise and ebb
To free them from silence or sorrowed pains?
Were they criminals, or tortured harshly for gains?
Or had there lived a maiden — loving and waiting?
Does her love story this crumbling relic store —
Disapproving kin and betrayal's footsteps grating?
Was it a cheery abode once, now shapeless in decay,
Or a den for lusty men, their victims led astray?
Musing thus, far and wide my thoughts spread.

Till the sand turned silver in this elixir of dream,
Astral jewels dancing with waves now grey,
Sat I, happily — my mind spinning stories supreme.
The ancient villa, in darkness, stored romance away.

Tales of love and hate, of jealousy and comparison—
Waiting to be gleaned in phantasmagoria's lore.
They could wait for discovery — for another time,
All the fables the house still holds in its core.

As the waves lash mightier, in bursts and in flurry,
They come, dancing wild — sudden, then slurry.
There will be morrows — O' iridescent stars, I take a bow.

Emotions

Smita Amit (1994)

Solace

Thou art my mother's arm—
Gentle warmth, unruffled calm,
Encompassing, ever-embracing,
My worries and troubles reducing.
Frail, yet firm—
Solace, thou art my mother's arm.

Pleasure

Thou art my companion's soft gaze—
Rosy sensations, an engulfing maze.
All excluding, we alone existing—
A rare moment, born of my longing,
Lasting but an ephemeral phase.
Pleasure, thou art my companion's soft gaze.

Pride

Thou art my child's excellence,
Scaling heights, horizons in radiance.
Toiling, stumbling, achieving—
My patience, my penance rewarding,
Shining, cascading brilliance.
Pride, thou art my child's excellence.

Pain

Thou art a wrenching parting,
Soul from the loved one's body departing.
Despair, as the patriarch leaves—
Gossamer shimmers, a white wreath,
Agonizing the fibre of life—hurting.
Pain, thou art a wrenching parting.

Eternity

Thou art the flowing stream,
A sliver of the moon, sunlight's beam.
I, in my progeny resurrecting—
In me, my parents reliving.
I that am, I that will be—
Eternity, thou art the flowing stream.

Contentment

Thou art as yet unknown,
Searching for thee, unturned no stone.
Idyllic fulfilment,
Gone all raging turbulence.
Lofty heart—thy worthy throne.
O Contentment, as yet unknown.

Ergo, They Wait

Smita Amit: 14/03/2010

Yonder, that gnarled stump—
Desolate, those naked trunks,
Jumbled-up branches like a child's scribbling—
A lonely heart's pining? Wailing or waiting?
I know not.

For it is that time o' the year,
When, in the early morning hours,
The trees—as is their wont—quiver.
But hark! Where is the rustle, sweet and clear?

It is naught—
For grieving heart, fall is here.
In all its glory—melancholy even—
When the streets lie covered
In yellow and green,
Calling for brooms once more to be clean.

In all this cessation,
The trees, patient, hardly ponder—
For once more will be those times
When the heavens open up,
And the skies verily change.
Ergo, they wait, stoically serene.

Kinks in the Armour

Smita Amit: 18/2/21

Kinks in the Armour
It seemed they had none —
Brave, valiant, indestructible —
They were steely men.
And yet there it was,
As clear as the day,
Each cursed with his own
Infinitesimal feet of clay.
Whether it be the frail,
Unprotected tender heel,
Left unwittingly bare —
Fate brought the hero to kneel.

Or the shining glory
Of locks in golden hue,
That cost a man his power —
A maiden's wile broke through.

Or the Lord's own command
That greenery obscure the light,
And the fabled mace found purchase —
Ending that undefeated fight.

Or he who bore the heavens,
Twelve labours his renown,
And yet in rage blind and raw

He struck his own blood down.
They who were gods in kind,
Still bore their flaw thus.

So why then seek perfection
In the mortals among us?
Though they may pose and prattle,
Their pride shall not allay—
The truth eternal, universal
They all have feet of clay.

If – A Woman's Cry

Smita Amit

At my feet, the world — in my palm, the vast sky,
If only, in this unequal world, as a man came I.
When but a few moons had crossed my eye,
And rare seasons in life had wondrously gone by,
Ignorant was the mind — any misgiving, faith did belie.

Conquering all, with virtue and beauty climbing high,
With all attributes God gave, to my best I did try.
But pointless was it all — worthless this bid to defy
The rules of men, where women just landscapes beautify.

Just working hands — no wings of fancy for her to fly.
Painfully have I learnt since, my role just to comply —
For I lost the race long ago, alas! With my first cry.

In Shambles...

Smita Amit: 6/4/21

So many, oh just so many a time,
As the clock strikes with a gloomy chime,
And the world around me lies dying,
With countless hordes for help crying.

When the order once known rapidly changeth,
And we crave once more that whiff of breath,
In shambles then, it all appears—
That which you built with sweat and tears.

You stand alone, betrayed, deceived,
Your innards raw, your soul aggrieved.
Shrieking surrounds—the hustle, the bustle,
Venom flies in every tussle.

Hark! There are still people spinning weaves vile,
For whom filth and bile are ever in style.
Some of them in it for profit's sake,
Some with hearts fit for the burning stake.

But wait—there are lessons hidden, aplenty,
That which shall toughen your core once dainty.
Tarry along, fight it out a bit longer,
That which does not kill makes you stronger.
So till the last breath, the last ounce, the last light—
Be brave, be cautious, and put up a worthy fight.
(inspired by covid-19)

Incarcerated

Smita Amit (March 2000)

A new beginning — tomorrow,
Will I surely see?
Gone, all sorrow,
My troubles will flee.

Tears of agony,
The heart once bled,
Becoming a blithe symphony —
All rapture spread.
The past would be burnished,
Glittering like gold.
My dreams would be fulfilled,
Opportunities manifold.

Head buried in my neck —
Thus do I live.
Interest not a speck
To my todays do I give.

So, drudgery my days,
Awaiting future.
Recalling a joyous time, now bygone —
Not charting new ways,
Or toiling for euphoric dawn.

The Edge of Forgiveness

Smita Amit (2002)

It is not easy to forget and forgive,
And to believe in you once again.
It is not easy to not again grieve
To get over the misery, the pain.

It is not easy my misgivings to leave,
And my trust in you to regain —
For when your guiding signals you receive,
You will wound me once again.

And yet, once more, I want to believe,
Semblance of a bond wishing to maintain —
Hoping you will no longer deceive,
Nor wrench me with words profane.
The seven vows not desiring to cleave,
My reticence hard to explain...
Fear of the unknown do I perceive,
Or is it love that does sustain?

Love ....

Smita Amit (Jan 2025)

Many posed the tangle, perplexed,
To define it — spent long hours, vexed.
The touch of the ineffable — gossamer,
Like velvet at dusk — for him, for her.

A promise to stay — bonds eternal,
Or a skipped heartbeat — fleeting, ephemeral.
"'Tis," said that, "it comes, goes unbridled —
A traveller mere yet strong-willed.

Roaming houses, towns — lane.
Coming, going — the joy, the pain.
Making some for a lifetime wait,
Or silken promises peeping at the gate."

A song that feels like home for some,
Or a nightmare in night, that never comes.
Is it caring — watchful waking in sickness
Amidst chaos — soft petals quaking their caress
Not asking permission, its right reclaiming —
Coming or going, many a ticker breaking.

Is it a play of chemicals merely,
As science proclaims, somewhat severely?
Or the pouring of self into the bond,
Like undelivered letters we grow fond

Of keeping — unopened, unsent,
Yet heavy with meaning and intent.
People have cried; many rejoiced —
Its coming, its going, in many a voice.

Artists — many, poets skilled,
In song or brush — pastel clouds filled —
Yet none could say, none could define
This dance of surrender, pure and divine.

So they wrote verses — inadequate, true,
But none could forget what it once drew.
By its magic, forever smote —
That silent ache behind every note.

Magic

Smita Amit: Feb 2021

The wistful mist—
A sigh caught in nature's throat,
Seen but not quite:
The outlines of the moored boat.

The whiff of engulfing fog
Carries the tale of faraway lands,
Floating the cotton clouds—
Like Oz with magical hands.

They seem heavy and ready to fall,
These billows travelling from afar,
Flying across lakes and peaks tall.

Damp and heavy,
The haze, with magic rife—
The peeping olive tops
Hide the straggling sigh of life.

Do nymphs, beauteous,
Dwell with elves and swishing mermaids,
Beyond the massive, impassive cliffs—
Silent glimmers in sap and ice shades?
The wisp of her golden locks
Beckons amidst the powdery blue,
Appealing to the suitor of faraway manors—

He, traversing the seven seas anew.
All is wondrous, charmed,
Colours hidden in the dripping cobalt.

There surely is a rainbow too,
Veiled in the watery treasure vault.
All seems touched
With the potion of wonder—
The puddle, the moors,
The vast mountain ranges yonder.

Yes, 'tis a miracle to live,
And stardust is all around—
With nature giving, and then some more...
The magic—it is bewitchingly profound.

O Just Sometimes

Smita Amit (1994/95)

There are times, O just sometimes,
Some odd moment, as the clock chimes—
My eyes go heavy, lids turn leaden,
Overtaken by the slumber of rejection.

My steady feet—
They start to falter,
And my load—
It gets hard to shoulder.

Trying hard, but never succeeding,
No dent in my fate creating.
Warmth gone, all covered by frost,
My shoulders sag—all seems lost.

Then I wish I were dust—
A whiff of air, a flake of rust,
Foam floating on the mighty wave,
A sliver of the morning haze.

A teeny bit amongst many a million—
There would be, then, no rebellion
Of spirit, or of mind;
One would I be, with many of a kind.
No distinction would I then seek.

My fate would I never bemoan, however bleak.
Born of obscurity—to the same returneth—
My plight I would never regret.

But nay! Human am I,
With a soul that never says die.
Dreams and hopes—all clustered,
Never by any failure flustered.
A mind with thought churning,
A heart with desires burning.

A spirit so very untiring,
With a will forever aspiring—
Reaching out to distant stars,
Even though the means be sparse.
Yearning for the alluding success,
Unfazed by all duress.

Striving ahead in a fashion brazen,
My struggle for utopia I never abandon—
Waiting and working for that coming dawn
When all would be bliss and troubles gone.
The warmth of love would fill my days,
The aura of success, showering praise.
Strange are the ways of the Lord—
My spirit survives of its own accord.
For that is what lies in me,
Deep down, where none can see—
The power to hope, the will to dream—
Indeed, me and my soul are a team!

Nature- the Eternal Mystic

Smita Amit (1993)

Inspired by the hills of Mussoorie / Dehradun

(1)

Translucent, mystic, ever advancing —
An invisible curtain, with time expanding.
Striving to see past, to hold and keep,
Eyes spellbound, through this I peep.
With abundant gaiety, a valley afar,
A dancing maiden, winks the periwinkle flower.
Enchanting mountains, abode of the Lord,
Scurrying rivulets — in haste they are shod.
The humming saplings, slightly bending,
Straggly pathways — unending.
Dunes of straw, a ship's lofty mast,
Gnarled stumps — eerie shadows cast.

(2)

Ticking slowly, my aeons are spent,
The curtain now drawn... night descends.
The spell is broken, my patterns jarred —
Bereft of glimpsing beauty, I stand scarred.
Lo! A music soft is filling the air,
Melodious stars driving away despair.
Shimmering, gleaming — the valley ablaze,

A princess's robe, that never does faze.
Grand lofty mountains, majestic, upright,
Spin stories of mystery and might —
Teaching a truth... long known to the wise,
To my soaring spirit and dancing eyes.

(3)

Eternal — the magic of nature's hue:
The waning dusk or the morning dew.
The aging adult, the child unborn,
The crafty hunter, the hapless fawn.
All are sagas of beauty — the Creator's ploy,
Displayed for us... these epics of joy.

You !!

Smita Amit (Nov 1993)

Who am I, or who are you —
Definitions many, fitting so few.
A teardrop upon the sands of time,
Or a sliver of feeling, deep, sublime.

In the maze of ties, a seeking cry,
Groping for a staff to steady all we try.
Hark! Your hand — who did ever hold?
When the world beckoned you in its fold?
Guided by instinct, you had come through,
Only will and strength you had with you.

Why then doth a kindred you seek,
In the teeming sea of men you meet?
They fell in step — some you met on the way,
Giving their company then, but a lifetime? Nay!
Your deeds are what, with you will go —
Or the way you dealt with friend or foe.

The hand you held of an ailing soul,
Or words you said that did console,
The smile you gave to lips distraught,
And blooms with which you replaced a draught.

Each sunshine ray that you diverged,
And hope in a man's heart you spurred —

They brought goodwill that weighs in gold,
And enriched your life — a treasure to hold.
Thus from all you see and all you learn,
A heart bejeweled is all you earn.
Square up then, with the skills you hone —
For life, its vagaries, are yours — and yours alone.

Fate Bends Not

Smita Amit 2015

Loving me truly, I wish were you,
'Twas not you who turned away,
I wish you had seen my pain.

Alas, fate bends not for what we do,
Nor molds a heart that will not stay—
And so, you walk through loss and rain.

Life was difficult, harsh, unkind,
A swan or butterfly you seemed—
Yet love is easier than the fight.

Commitment faded like morning wind,
You chased the stars, a fleeting dream,
And fled before they burned too bright.

The past has left me scarred and torn,
My trials began at a tender age,
Yet life went on—no time to dwell.

Much later, when our paths were worn,
No longing bound me in a cage;
For life had kept me busy well.

Maybe as kin, you'd come to be, I thought,
Well past the thrill, now steady, wise—
Yet you blamed me squarely for the past.

You stirred up guilt, my heart was caught,
Yearning to break time's cold ties,
As fog upon my mind was cast.

Grave my plight—could you ever fathom
That time of guilt, of doubt unspoken?
My mind adrift on waves too wide.

Upset was life, yet duty-bound—wholesome—
Your voice, your wit, a fire awoken,
Yet sadly, you would not abide.

Painting me the wrongdoer still,
You turned away, refused our love to see.
Who was wronged—you, or me?
My weakness bent to suit your will,
Unanswered yearnings, like tides at sea,
Drifting far, yet never free.

O' Autumn

Smita Amit

O' Autumn,
From whence comes this pall—
This pain, this ache that holds in thrall
My spirit—my very being, snow-showered,
As if jest ebbs, blow by blow, devoured?
Is it the leaves of autumn shredding?
Or the dry air, my insides kneading?

Is it the time of trials prevailing—
That saps me up—my soul, unfailing?
Why this despondence? Why the gloom
Amidst such riotous, resplendent bloom?

What makes my heart yearn long—
From where springs this melancholy song?
O' Autumn, thou dost sadden my numbles true,
With beauty stark, in burnt orange hue.
The crunching leaves, the blowing wind—
All dreams, all hopes... alas, rescind.

On the Train, Once Again

Smita Amit (2010)

Like a ship at sea, with the wind in its sails,
Knowing not what lies ahead, nor what tomorrow entails
Just me, my fantasies, liberated from domestic grind,
Winking at the derelict stable on the way, the sallow blind.

My train chugs busily, rhythmically westward bound,
I find my childhood peeping from somewhere around.
As I look out, finding roads where there were none,
The abounding cement monsters — many more than one.

The birds and trees fewer, few shrubs, fewer the trees,
But the soil, all gold, still flirts charmingly with the breeze.
The land unknown calls still, like the brook gentle and mild,
The winding, lonely mud tracks still give the call of the wild.

Much has changed an era, even but has it all gone really by?
For the journey, the quest, all remain... I still want to away fly.

And Yet She Waited

Smita Amit 2019

There was silver in her hair,
Once lissom, the back was bent with care.
The fingers gnarled—those once supine,
A whimpering stream, no longer the Rhine.

And yet she waited.
Waited by the window bay,
Come hail or storm or the fever of hay.
The lustrous, limpid, large eyes so fetching—
Today, just under the glasses, stretching.

And yet she waited.
With bated breath scarcely apart,
Waited near the doorway of her heart.
A lump in the throat, missing many a beat,
Startled, her reverie by the patter of each feet.

And yet she waited.
Waited for the rainbow bridge to heal,
For her fate to miraculously anneal.
The dimpled chin that had bewitched many and more,
Seemed today food for reminiscence and lore.

And yet she waited.
Waited for the promised fairy-tale
Of roses and candies and ginger ale.

With the slipper of glass, delicate and fine,
She got bleary-eyed waiting by the violet vine.

And yet she waited.
Scarlet flickering from whence bit the thimble,
Her toiling hands no longer nimble.
At the foyer of her fate she sat—
Would ever the skies hear her caveat?

And yet she waited.
With winter in her soul, waiting for spring,
Some time, some galaxy, beyond the fiery ring.
In an elusive Arcadia beyond the universe' shore,
They would be one—she and her Thor.

For years had she waited,
And for the remaining, she will—
Awaiting her Thor forever more,
Waiting for Thor forever more.

Looking for Bliss

Smita Amit (2000)

Laughing and singing, on dancing feet
Carefree footsteps, prancing on the street
Hand in hand as it sailed with thunder —
I envied the rain, beauteous in its splendor.

So, like the dreamy younger, bygone days,
Naïve and trusting — so far from my todays.
All utopia, the world a rosy pink,
The twilight, morn written in magical ink.
Hopes, aspiration, and many a dream —
All attainable, it did then seem.

Young, and not yet seen any dismay —
Sadly, it did happen along the way.
The pitter and patter of rain was lost,
My whole world sort of covered with frost.
Shattered dreams, aspirations blown away,
Icy winds of disenchantment holding sway.

Clipped wings now — the soaring spirit aggrieved,
Wondering what happened, befuddled and peeved.
Realization came then, though a bit late —
I had grown up, encountering my fate.

Life, oh! is but a troublesome commodity,
And the world's not rosy — just irksome duty.

Dreams a load, never coming true —
Illusions vanishing, with not a clue.
Where does then the essence, the beauty lie?
Is there much more to it than meets the eye?
How does one make the best out of this —
And steer life's ship forward to bliss??

Reincarnation

Smita Amit · 2/10/24

When I go—and I will—
Will it be a zero thereafter,
Or something greater still,
That carries the tears, the laughter?

The gross body of the elements five
Will, with the Fire God, have its date.
My subtle one—will it remain alive?
Will the causal one still not disintegrate?
Am I just a program on a machine,
Bound to this realm—earthly, gross, unseen?
Expendable matter, fated to abort—
Or a being hidden in this fort,
A soul for whom the divine has import?
Did I live before? And will I once more?
Is there a way to learn this for sure?

Silence

Smita Amit

The silence of sound,
And the sound of silence.
Speaking without words—profound,
In the weakest moments: resilience.
The language of the mind,
And the mind in all languages.

The dogmas that my soul did bind—
All gone, their signage.
Expression in all art,
And the art of expression.

The mind hidden in the heart,
The heart soaking —validation.
Such is the beauty of nature,
And such is the nature of beauty—
Unsullied, basking in the Creator's nurture,
Permanent its brilliance, not fleetly.

Stifled

Smita Amit (Feb 2021)

Stifled,
She breathed for years, many—
Routines dragged on, turmoil uncanny.
Was it
Intellect struggling, hence,
Or was it her mind endeavoring to make sense?

Was it hope
That pulled the cart,
Though disillusions bayed to pull it all apart?
Was it youth,
Seeing all with a tint rosy,
That made her make from troubles a dainty posy?

There were days, true,
She sat at the precipice dark—
Between bondage and release calling, hark!
To live for—
There were lives young,
So she chose her hard, soothing, her nerves strung.
She toiled for them,
The proverbial mother hen;
Slowly spreading wings, they flew... it hit her then:
Why did she ne'er her fate defy?
Why no dream did she dream, ever?

The toil for her own joy—why did she do never?
Today, at life's twilight,
Nothing matters—the drudgery, the strife.
All that was is now a blur: mere memory of being alive.
Her eyes are pools still—
They that had been pools twinkling ebullience,
Today though, they are still, with sheathed turbulence.
All she wants
Is to fly away—free, far beyond,
Into her grandma's never-land, with lotus and frond.

Silhouette's

Smita Amit: 4/10/24

O, were I the princess of the atom,
A lady widely sought after —
Regal, beauteous — a blossom,
With loads of joy and laughter.

But no hair-brained dame am I,
Holding together my creed, my clan.
In the lineage of kings — no fly-by,
Ruling bravely, with vigorous élan.

Maybe to earth I was spirited away
By some villainous hand, vile schemes.
Maybe evil gained, held sway —
One moment, how true it seems.

The next — what if, I was just a slug,
Of a giant being's tiniest part —
A speck of dust, a nit, even a bug,
What if I have no end, no start?
What if I am an illusion mere,
Neither giant nor Lilliput?
Hark! the thoughts are queer,
And in my mouth the foot is put.

Tales and Lessons – The Web

Smita Amit: 13/07/25

For hours many, in patience it labours on,
One thread delicate, another laid upon.
Tensile, elastic, possessing great strength,
Radial, symmetrical in its width and length.

The natural orb the creature weaves,
The prey ensnared, its lifeblood it leaves.
Once in this web, helplessly it struggles,
Waiting afar — the predator as the tremor gurgles.

The prince, young, valiantly went in,
Murdered he was by sly kith and kin.
But exit path unknown, untold
To him — as an unborn, his mother's fold.

The structure man made, with vile intent,
Mighty kings in avarice, their conscience bent.
This web, alas! he could not penetrate—
Many say it was deceit, others, his fate.

Modern man, he — the pseudo-wise,
Building strange platforms, precise yet unkind.
The web smiles back — an echo thin,
Where secrets stay, though visible within.

It never forgets, never erases,
The memory remains hidden in places.
Sharing your life on this web created,
Many suffer, feeling bereft, cheated.

And then the master schemer —
The one who lays the trap for many a dreamer.
Or the one who creates the mighty code,
That can destroy kingdoms, kings' abode.

In such webs — seemingly harmless or vile,
In the mind that spins nets many a mile,
He who spun it finds himself caught,
Struggling to untangle, its efforts worth naught.

Many are webs, natural or man-made,
Giving misery to the boy or the lissome maid.
But is it really impossible, fruitless,
To escape from the web that seems limitless?

The exit unknown to the warrior's brave son,
But it was there — for all webs have one.
Knowledge, persistence, strength, or stealth
Can break the web, giving freedom wealth.

The Childhood Still Waits

Smita Amit (27 June 2020)

The vast, placid blue—
Mysterious, unending,
Hermetic, it beckons,
Shimmering, the colour of dew.

They say a kingdom lies
Buried deep within,
A realm well-heeled and ample,
Suspiring, its sorrows it hides.

The mist that I was, I flew
Atop the bewitching lake.
There were the sobs, the sighs—
But the entrée I did not pursue.

They had a story to tell
Of long-gone colonies that thrived,
Tales of loving and losing,
Of how the calamity befell.

But I laughed with the ducks, teal,
As they swam in a row,
Caressing the blooming lotuses—
The lost kingdom did not appeal.

The gust of wind that I was, I swerved
And entered the nearby woods,
Whooshing through the trees evergreen—
I made merry, though they soughed.

Billowing thus, as a stream, I enter my ear,
Striking a note multihued—
A symphony, a whistle, an eerie sound,
A whisper or a trumpet's blare.

And with wonder, I look above—
The stars, they take me afar.
As a princess that I was, I wheezed past,
My atom world a treasure trove.

Manoeuvring down its tunnels in spate,
My lustrous automobile on winds—
Near the bushes by the lake,
My kind, my subjects, hopefully I await.

Though years passed and worlds changed,
Reason was taught, and sensibility was learnt—
Yet between logic and magic, next to the gates,
The childhood—unaware—still waits.

The Day the Song Died

Smita Amit (2015)

Was it autumn—
Spring? Winter even?
Scant memory now,
Faint its fragrance.

Wispy remembrance
Like gathered pearls,
Her cache of songs
From the cord of life—
Ready to fly today,
Break free, drift away.

Unexpected it came then:
Gossamer light,
Susurration, a murmur—
That thought, caressing,
Winged, and charming.

Fie, that gay abandon—
The song of her prancing feet,
Twittering, unmindful
On the road muddy, slick
At each askew brick.

With folded hands,
As the assembly followed,

A song she sang—
All decorous and prim,
Her joy though full to the brim.
Sitting, chatting
On the carpet of green—
Crooning blades
Twirled in her fingers,
Soulful sweet jingles.

Radiant like a rainbow,
Song of a mynah
On the swing,
Her body in flight—
Feathery and light.

They had walked together,
Young and in love,
From a gate to the other,
In emotion each step—
In melody singing, hippety-hep.
Now a mother,
The beloved long gone,
Doting sweet joys
Gurgling along—
Honeyed, her cradle song.
Moments had flown.

Songs of her bruises—
Melancholy now,
Nineteen to a dozen,

Sang of the vacuum within.
Years later—
Irrevocable, they all exist:
The swing that goes to and fro,
The slick, the gates, the green,
Winking with their glean.

But no song exists today,
Foretasting no morrow—
Notes, sad nor low,
No expression of joy,
No yearning her feelings cloy.

The tune has flown,
So has the melody.
The nectar in the jingle—
Woefully dried.
And a song unknown died.

The twinkle—
It flew away then,
When the vacant heart
Neither laughed nor cried.
That is the day the song died.

Ruins

Smita Amit (1998)

---

(1)

Alluring, like a rosebud, winsome, light
Resplendent in toil, gearing to sprite
A bubble of energy, reacting, buoyant
Like notes on a flute, pulsating, vibrant
A shimmering prism, blinding, aglow
A bounding river, unrestrained, its flow
And engrossed, in me, my strength
Haughtily my time, I vainly spent
Tho' it was you, that made me ... me
Without you, would I me be?

(2)

Uncomplaining, ye stood by me as one
Tho' waking moments for you I spared none
No inkling of you, no respect even
Lacking about you all acumen
You however tarried along unfazed
Friend, ally, mentor — you have me amazed
My spirit, I wonder what makes you thus
My stout companion, staying without a fuss?
For it was you, that made me ... me
Without you, would I me be?

(3)

Destiny intervenes, alas! time stings
Like the flash of the eyelid, you take wings
Gone ... departed forever
All ties with me, then you sever
I remain a deflated bubble, no pep, no zing
A broken flute, a listless being
Desolate entire, leaden, a has-been
A shattered prism with no sheen
Alas! it was you, that made me ... me
Without you, how could I me be?

(4)

Just a name, an epitaph
On one corner, a framed photograph
Adorned with jewels once a moment past
Now the snapshot decks the walls vast
Dust to dust, ashes to ashes — all sprite divest
Inert, static — in eternal rest
Now you have left, to realms one knows not
And a lonely family remains bereaved, lost
For you alone had made me ... me
The sprightly me, now I can no longer be. (2)

The Bleeding Heart

Smita Amit (1991)

Secure — like in a violin, its chord,
Years ago, it was that close to the Lord.
Then it was so serenely white,
Not sullied by rancour nor any spite.

As time passed, adding the years,
Plagued it was by many fears.
Tears of agony, alas, it shed —
Torn by strife, it slowly bled.
The white became then dotted with red,
As a little of its hopes away they sped.

The kiss of life sustains yet —
All desires, their death not yet met.
Sparkling emeralds of blissful green
Dull the red with alluring sheen.

Sparsely placed in small packages,
They are some joys and fulfilled wishes.
Scattered along — the white, the green, and red,
The blows felt, and smiles spread.
The joys and sorrows their colours impart,
Swaying, slaying — the bleeding heart.

The Dive

Smita Amit July 2025

Crafted over time, tools that stare
Deep within the tiny cell—
For man to see and dwell
On the smallest truths laid bare.

Others developed to grossly magnify,
To tell man what lies far beyond—
Be it beasts, or lakes, or frond
Of stars that in black silence lie.

His quest never ultimate, complete,
In each decade as a new truth emerges,
A better tool, more probing all edges—
But alas, the knowledge cart with holes replete.

As man peers into the minuscule,
Unravels the gigantic stars he strives,
In the big or small fruitlessly he dives,
Struggling, eroding all his tool.

But they in meditation calmly sat,
Saints—exalted souls of old—
The Creation, its mysteries then did unfold,
To them on their simple grass mat.

Deep within the recesses of their mind,
They schooled the chit to probe within—
For the soul knows all if you quiet the din,
In its connection to the universe's net, all rescinds.

They knew the origin, they knew the sound,
Distances between stars, their annihilation-birth,
Multiverse—or many a earth—
They knew it all, how lokas abound.

Alas! Some conquered, looted, destroyed,
The voice of the ancients buried quiet.
Dimmed their knowledge that once burned bright,
Some who stole, in erroneous decoding employed.

But the truth remains that- forever more,
And try as he might, the crafty man will n'er arrive
For ultimate they gained—as inside was their dive—
The men mighty, now gone, remain just folklore.

The Nilgiris

Smita Amit (1994)

Beauteous—
Exalted, yet soft.
Mist—
Ethereal, gently wafts.

Lustrous—
Their coat of green.
Ranges—
Lofty, calm, serene.

Hutments—
And quaint hamlets.
Idyllic—
Red and white huts.

Peaks—
Veiled in mystery.
Behold—
The enigmatic Nilgiris.

Charisma—
Enthralling all and sundry.
Blue mist—
Thy crowning glory.

The Knot in My Temple

Smita Amit (20/9/2001)

Inspired by a mother's story during the Twin Towers blast

The knot in my temple —
It refuses to go away.

The lead perched on my heart
Makes it unsteadily sway.
Disquiet floods my thoughts —
Alas! in a mad disarray.

Where art thou, my loving son?
Trepidation strips hope away.
Did you escape the wrath of time,
Miraculously slip away?

Or, caught like many fellowmen,
Do you beneath the rubble lay?
The mind, now refusing to think,
Repeats — *nay! nay! nay!*

Violence in Me

Smita Amit (1999)

In me it is not—
Thus, I always thought.
It is... in them,
Causing all the mayhem.

But then, who are *they*?
If not, people like me—pray?
Animal instinct, they call it,
Giving all manly excesses a clean chit.

Violence that is in me
Is deep—none can see,
Simmering always,
Guiding many of my ways.

Out... it surfaces,
Destroying—it blazes.
When I hurt my bride,
Basking in masculine pride,
It gushes out like rain—
And I, unfeelingly, restrain
Her dreams, her desires,
Stoking my own fires.

Her—as I try to subdue,
I maim her, 'tis true.
To my wishes she does not surrender—
Ruthlessly and savagely… I burn her.

A wailing child
By the roadside
Tugs at my heart,
And relief I instantly impart.

But my sobbing wife,
So overcome with strife—
I neither see nor console,
Unmindful of her, as a whole.

She rejects my decree—
How dare she!
I then tear her to shreds,
Words destroying the vows sacred.
And yet, am I violent?
No.

And I never repent.
For I am a man—
Born in the superior clan.
To quell is my right,
'Cause I win with my might.
As born, I am to subjugate,
Servitude and tears—her fate.

So, violence now remains
No longer *in* us humans.
It is now an animal instinct.
In *us*, it is... long extinct. (2)

The Martyr

Smita Amit (1999)

An ambush it was —
That which made him *It.*
Desolation they did cause,
The bullets that hit.

Motionless, his body
Lies encased in white.
The father, with eyes ruddy,
Bereft of all sprite.

Free — the valiant soul,
From all worldly confines,
Paying a heavy toll —
A sister's heart pines.

The motherland defending
Went the apple of her eye.
The mother's agony, unending:
Why did she not also die?

His own mother, shattered,
Pillaged — her loving hand.
Sons like him, stout-hearted —
Many has the motherland.

No Throw for Her

Smita Amit, 20/1/2025

Draupadi, who was she really?
A princess, fire-born.
Wronged—or a woman steely?
Lotuses blue, fragrance adorn
Her beauteous tender frame—
Unparalleled even, ornaments shorn.

Was she a docile dame,
Her husbands only pleasing?
Surely she was not so tame.
From flames she—arising,
Not wanted, no mother even—
A tool for her father everlasting.

Wedded by heroic men,
Brothers they—all of five,
Exiled for years two and ten.
Many trials she did survive.
To save her honour, ventured none—
The Lord her glory kept alive.

Her husbands, the great war won.
Many say it was her vengeance creed,
Instigating—she was the one.
All of this—in history feed.

Easy to look up, wonder,
If the books, ancient, you read.
But between all this thunder,
Who, after all, was she—
Refusing steadfastly to surrender?
Unassuming, never could be,
Nor a naive wife either—
Strange for her—fate's decree.

Turmoils never giving a breather,
Whom, if any, out of five she loved?
Or did they love her neither?
A song of pure love ever hummed,
Or a life of shackling duty?
Who did to her of the five belonged?
Taking other wives—plenty.

Her sons—killed, avenged never.
Of what use her greatness, beauty?
The victim of a plot clever.
Did her heart bleed and lament,
Or was she stoic, heroic forever?
Though godliness—her armament,
Yet born a woman she was—
The nymph, lotus-eyed, unique scent.

Obeying all earthly laws,
Was she a goddess divine,
Not beset by human flaws?
They say three deities did combine,

And her—the exquisite—make.
She never could say: *He is mine.*
She, who duty never did forsake—
The valiant, brave, astounding woman
Whom the husband for the dice did stake.

The Legacy

Smita Amit (1998)

Inspired by the death of a young mother in army circles who gave birth to her child despite having cancer

Reigning supreme, reverberating — silence.
The atmosphere grim, the air dense.

They paced the floor, their pulses wild —
One could be saved: the mother or child.
Like lightning across a darkened sky,
Broke forth, at last, an infant's cry —
A newborn eager to know the earth,
His race, his land, his home and hearth.
The mother lay — all spent, all prone,
Yet abundant joy in her heart shone.
But the pain — it gnawed at her core;
Death was near. She'd fight no more.

And yet, here was her little one,
Flesh of her flesh, her infant son.
Snuggled safe in the crook of her arm,
She tried to shield him from all harm.

He lay at peace, no hint of fear,
But the mother's heart was rent with despair.
She looked from him to the skies above,
Imploring the Gods with a mother's love:
Pulling her child close to her heart,

She whispered thus, her legacy's start:
"O blood of my blood, my darling son,
To give to you, possessions — I have none.

To rock you to sleep in the hours wee —
Alas, my arms shall never be.
To tell you of fairies and bunnies who flew,
Of birds that swam, and fishes too...

I, your mother, will not be there,
But I'll help you still — do not despair.
For the blood in you that comes from me
Will guide you through life's stormy sea.

I may not share your joys or sorrows,
Nor see your todays or tomorrows,
And yet, what you learned in my womb
Will help you stride past fear and gloom.

I may not teach you to run or play,
But I've taught you to find your way.
For I have tutored you to survive,
To strive in pain, and rise alive.
Braving all odds, the grief, the strain,
I've borne you forth through mortal pain.

Fighting my ailment, unseen, unheard,
I gave you life — my final word.
A kingdom, no, I cannot give,
But from me, you have learned to live.

Stoutness of heart I've passed to you —
For you are a fighter, strong and true.
In the coming hours, I shall be gone,
Myself, my habits — but echoes, anon.
And yet, within you, I will live on —
Though I may not see the coming dawn."

Strength

Smita Amit

A rivulet, a river — a sea, even —
Escaped my lids and scurried on.
Was there ever a kindred soul
To water the drought in my heart? Never.
Watch me drown in that sea,
Thrash and tear asunder my being —
My air: hunger.
A desert of emotions trailing behind,
Watered by my own sea —
Did a kind soul I ever find?
They capture the moment in their reels,
Not to save, but to nudge me down —
To sink, to perish.
Ah, how many wait to dance
In ruins they long to see enhanced.
But I — I am my sail.
These hands, my staff.
My faith, my anchor;
My mind, my craft.
With these, I build my palace of dreams,
A story worthy of ink and reams.
To accord them privilege?
To assuage their hunger?
No —
I was not made to surrender.

My Tryst with Poetry and Prose

Smita Amit: 27-06-24

There are some who are born *feeling...*
What exactly, you may ask—
The smile, the sigh, the upswing or the reeling
Of thoughts distraught, or in joy that bask.

Every moment, they are there,
To define them? An uphill task.
I felt the wind. I felt the rain.
I felt the greens. I felt the brown.

The joy in waves, in lofty mountains—their pain.
I just had my feelings—no twinkle, no frown.
Thus started a journey, a calling, you may say.

The beggar woman, the Nilgiris, the gnarled tree stump—
They beckoned me, their feelings to assay.
The pandemic, however, brought a welcome hump.

And that which was brief, succinct, and lyrical
Came back again -novellas, rhymes soothing and *Sheer*—
The world of contemplation—gripping, magical,
Affairs of the heart, to me so dear.

But is that all that is me, I ponder
Am I this body, this mind, or me?
If it's me, then who- O! wonder?
Can anyone this me see?
A hand is lost or two
The voice lost or the sight
Yet I remain me, not you
Yet me in me remains there-tight
A heart replaced or the liver
In my dreams, I roam, I swim over skies
Yet my -me changes - never
Though the face, the body, not seeing my eyes
I am me - that a finality
This makes me think again and again
Even in that alternate, strange reality
Does the body have me or the body I contain (2)